COVENANT CHRONICLES

COVENANT CHRONICLES

EXEGETICAL EXPLORATIONS OF THE BAPTIST CHURCH COVENANT

Jarvis J. Hanson, Sr.

Urban Publishing House, LLC

Legacy Hardback ISBN: 979-8-8693-8763-9
Paperback ISBN: 979-8-3303-3730-9
EBook - Founder's Special Ediiton, Only at UPH and Dr. Hanson's Ministry Venues

First Published by Urban Publishing House, LLC, 2024
"Authors Who Write with Integrity, Intelligence, and Inspiration"
P.O. Box 742
Oxnard, CA 93032
1-888-671-2922
www.urbanpublishinghouse.com
admin@urbanpublishinghouse.com

DEDICATION

To my beloved wife, Dr. Brandy Lynn, and our precious children, Alycen-Grace and Jarvis Jr., whose love and unwavering support are the bedrock upon which stand. Your presence in my life is a daily reminder of God's grace and favor.

To my dear parents, Donald Hanson Sr. and Alice, who have been my first teachers and lifelong examples of faith, love, and perseverance. Your sacrifices and prayers have paved the way for everything I have become.

To my cherished siblings, Veronica, Rev. Donald Jr. (Latrisha), and Kwasi Sr. (Jessica), your support, wisdom, and camaraderie have been pillars of strength throughout my journey.

To my nieces, nephews, aunts, uncles, cousins, and my family in love, your love and encouragement have enriched my life beyond measure.

To my family, friends, and my brothers and sisters in the gospel, especially "The GoodFellas," your steadfast encouragement and companionship have been a source of strength and inspiration. Together, we have navigated the valleys and climbed the mountains of this journey.

To the congregation of New Nazareth Missionary Baptist Church, where I am blessed to serve as pastor, your faith and trust in me are both a sacred respon-

sibility and a divine gift. And to my home church, United Faith Missionary Baptist Church, where my roots are deep, thank you for nurturing my calling and continually lifting me in prayer.

To the Greater New Era Baptist District Association, the Baptist General State Convention of Illinois, and The National Baptist Convention USA, Inc., I am profoundly grateful for the opportunities to serve within these esteemed bodies. The fellowship we share is a testament to our collective commitment to the work of the Kingdom.

Special thanks to the founder of Urban Publishing House, LLC, Pastor Derrick I. Temple, Sr., whose support and belief in this work have been instrumental in bringing this vision to life. Your encouragement has been both a guiding light and a sustaining force.

#Kerusso

FOREWORD-Rev. Dr. A. Edward Davis, Jr.

I would like to take this moment to commend Dr. Jarvis Hanson for compiling a concise translation of the Baptist Church Covenant. Living in this society in which there is so much instability, so many have various interpretations and vacillate in their Baptist Doctrine.

Allow me to say, "We are Baptist by denomination." I am amazed that many do not know the structure of biblical teaching that the covenant we make is with God, and we do not understand our covenantal relationship with the Church. Dr. Hanson has put together a concise translation of the biblical Covenant of the Church.

I would like to thank my spiritual son for being led to put together such a concise and clear understanding of the meaning of the Covenant with God and the relationship with the Church.

- Rev. Dr. A. Edward Davis, Jr.
Pastor, St. John Missionary Baptist Church
Chicago, Illinois

FOREWORD-Rev. Dr. James Flint, Jr.

From our Baptist Faith, we have had many who branched-off into other lines of biblical thinking, and expressed "religious freedom" to leave our beloved tradition, never to acknowledge our core foundation again. At the same time, many have also reached to recreate a system that undeniably reverts back to a Baptist model, mission, and message.

Then, we have this new paradigm, which appears to happen only in our setting, where there has been a breach by other faith traditions to come into our Baptist churches and systematically endeavor to uproot and dismantle the tenants we fundamentally hold so dear. This too, is coupled with an uprising of uneducated leaders, impatient, and unmotivated to trace the line of historical accounts. Many of us know this is necessary to gain access to the keys of local church restoration, the sustainability of community engagement, and the advancement of God's Kingdom.

The voice of the Baptist Church that was once thunderous and intentional has softened to slightly over a whisper, and has been relegated to congregational confinement while there is a world in need of a consciousness of our Christ and His Cross. Roles have been reversed in many of our circles of faith, in that now, the world impresses upon us its program instead of us, as the Church, impressing God's program upon the world. I truly believe this is because we have allowed the currents of today's climate to cause us to drift away from the shore of our convictions regarding Jesus Christ and our Great Commission.

There is a need for us to be re-calibrated, reminded, and theologically reinvested in the rudiments of our tradition.

Covenant Chronicles is an essential and necessary composition for any serious steward of the Gospel serving in any station of the Baptist Faith. It has obviously been steeped in diligent prayer, the searching of scripture, and profound study. Its movement will captivate, inspire, and equip you to respond to the world through a Baptist lens as you aim to live out your faith highlighting the *Grace of God*, the *Love of Christ*, and the *Communion of the Holy Spirit*.

I am grateful to Dr. Hanson for this needful piece of scholarship, and I am thankful to him for surrendering to the voice of God in dedicating his time to this project and sharing with us this missive for Baptist ministry.

-Rev. Dr. James Flint, Jr.
Pastor, Calvary Baptist Church
Chicago, Illinois

FOREWORD-Rev. Dr. J. Michael Tennial

As I reflect on my journey through the corridors of faith, there is a constant thread that weaves through my earliest memories of church life—the Church Covenant. Etched boldly on the walls of New Zion City Baptist Church in Chicago, Illinois, where I spent my formative years, I was licensed and ordained to the Gospel Ministry, and boldly spoken aloud during solemn moments of communion at Concord Baptist Church of Christ in Brooklyn, the Covenant has been a silent witness to my spiritual growth.

I vividly recall tracing its words with curious fingers as a child, pondering their meaning in the dim light of the sanctuary. It was a declaration—a promise—etched in scriptural language, binding together generations of believers in commitment to each other and to God. I remember the hushed reverence in the congregation when the Covenant was read aloud, its clauses becoming a rhythmic heartbeat of our shared faith.

It was not until later, amidst the bustling streets and diverse tapestry of Brooklyn, that I truly grasped the profound significance of this Covenant. Serving as Pastor in Residence at Concord Baptist Church of Christ, I witnessed firsthand how the Covenant formed the moral and spiritual backbone of our community. Around the communion table, as we reaffirmed our commitment to God and each other, I realized that the Covenant was not just words on paper but a living testament to our faith in action.

In *COVENANT CHRONICLES*, my dear friend Jarvis J. Hanson embarks on a journey of exegetical exploration into the Church Covenant—a cornerstone of belief in many Black Baptist Churches across our nation. Jarvis's dedication to Baptist doctrine is unparalleled, his scholarly insights a beacon for those seeking to understand not just what we believe, but why we believe it. Through meticulous research and deep reverence for scripture, he unveils the layers of meaning embedded in these timeless words, illuminating their relevance for today's believers.

In an age where doctrine is sometimes viewed as rigid or outdated, Jarvis reminds us of the beauty found in understanding and affirming our beliefs. *COVENANT CHRONICLES* is more than a scholarly work; it is a heartfelt invitation to delve into the spiritual treasures that lie within our shared heritage. As Baptists, knowing what we believe and why is paramount, and Jarvis Hanson's work is a timely guidepost for this journey of discovery.

I commend this book to you not just as an introduction to the Baptist Church Covenant, but as a testament to the faithfulness of God and the enduring power of community. May it inspire you, as it has inspired me, to embrace with renewed vigor the promises we make to God and to one another.

- Rev. Dr. J. Michael Tennial
  Chicago, Illinois

FOREWORD-Rev. Dr. Davie L. Moore

It is with great pleasure and honor that I have the privilege to write the Foreword of *Covenant Chronicles: Exegetical Explorations of the Church Covenant.* As a long-time friend, colleague, and admirer of Dr. Hanson, I have witnessed firsthand, his unwavering commitment to the church and his passion for sharing the wisdom and teachings of the Gospel.

Throughout his many years of service as a husband, father, preacher, and pastor, Dr. Hanson has exemplified the true essence of leadership. His dedication to the spiritual growth and well-being of the church at large has been nothing short of inspiring, and his ability to articulate and interpret the teachings of the Word of God and the Church Covenant is unparalleled.

In *Covenant Chronicles,* Dr. Hanson delves deep into the intricacies of the Church Covenant, offering exegetical explorations that are both enlightening and thought-provoking. His insightful analysis and profound understanding of the Covenant will undoubtedly provide readers with a deeper appreciation and understanding of this fundamental aspect of church life.

Dr. Hanson's writing is not only informative but also deeply reflective of his own personal journey and experiences within the church community. His words are imbued with wisdom, compassion, and a genuine desire to guide and inspire others on their own spiritual paths.

I have no doubt that *Covenant Chronicles* will serve as a valuable resource for church leaders, members, and anyone seeking a deeper understanding of the Church Covenant. Dr. Hanson's expertise, passion, and dedication shine through in every page, making this book a must-read for all those who are committed to the spiritual growth and well-being of their communities.

It is my sincere hope that this book will touch the hearts and minds of all who read it, and that Dr. Hanson's profound insights will continue to inspire and guide us in our own spiritual journeys.

- Rev. Dr. Davie L. Moore

Pastor, Greater New Mount Eagle
Chicago, Illinois

ADVANCED PRAISE-Endorsements

COVENANT CHRONICLES is the mature fruit of a dedicated and devout young scholar. Here, Jarvis J. Hanson weaves theory, passion, and practice together into a rich representation of the Baptist Church Covenant. He takes the discussion of the Covenant Chronicles which is grounded in biblical principles and mirrors it with scripture so the church can shift the emphasis from private pursuit to corporate congregational culture.

This book is loaded with Biblical Church Discipline that will shape the character and conduct of a believer that will transform a church that represent the life of Jesus Christ. I encourage every church and its members to use COVENANT CHRONICLES as a tool to mature and grow to the fullest of Christ.

-Rev. Dr. William H. Foster, Jr.

Senior Pastor, Providence Baptist Church of Chicago, Illinois; Vice-President of the Midwest Region-National Baptist Convention USA, Inc.; Immediate Past President of The Baptist General State Convention of Illinois

* * *

In an era where the essence of community and shared faith can often be overshadowed by the busyness of our lives, this book stands as a beacon, illuminating the profound significance of our spiritual bonds and commitments.

Drawing from deep theological insights and personal reflections, Rev. Dr. Jarvis Hanson unravels the layers of the church covenant, highlighting its enduring relevance and transformative power. This book is not just a scholarly exploration; it is a heartfelt invitation to rediscover the covenant's roots and its implications for our collective journey of faith. Enjoy the read,

- Rev. A. William Staten, Jr.

Pastor, Alpha Temple Baptist Church Englewood
Chicago, Illinois

* * *

Endorsing a book as profound and timely as COVENANT CHRONICLES by Pastor Jarvis Hanson is both an honor and privilege. In an era where doctrinal clarity and covenantal faithfulness are more crucial than ever, Pastor Hanson has masterfully provided a beacon of wisdom and insight for the contemporary church.

COVENANT CHRONICLES meticulously explores the Baptist Church Covenant, offering a fresh, theologically rich, and accessible perspective that is bound to enrich both seasoned theologians and lay believers, alike. Pastor Hanson's adept handling of doctrinal issues is not merely academic; it is deeply pastoral, resonating with the heart of every reader who longs to see the church thrive in fidelity to its commitments.

Pastor Hanson combines thorough biblical scholarship with practical application, making this work an indispensable resource for those seeking to understand and live out the covenantal principles that have long defined Baptist faith and practice. His writing is both inspiring and convicting, encouraging readers to embrace the full depth of their covenantal relationship with God and with one another.

Covenant Chronicles is a timely reminder of the strength found in doctrinal unity and the power of living in covenant with our Creator. Pastor

Hanson's passion for the church and his commitment to sound doctrine shine through on every page, making this book not only a must- read but also a transformative experience.

I wholeheartedly endorse Covenant Chronicles and believe it will serve as a cornerstone resource for churches, pastors, and believers who seek to deepen their understanding of the Baptist Church Covenant and to live out their faith with integrity and purpose. Pastor Hanson has truly given the church a gift that will impact generations to come.

- Rev. Dr. Claude L. White Jr.

Pastor, Grace Baptist Church
Peoria, Illinois

* * *

Within a remarkably dynamic contemporary Black Baptist Church, Reverend Dr. Jarvis Hanson offers a traditional doctrinal perspective that largely defined a golden age of Black religious experience. In COVENANT CHRONICLES, Dr. Hanson provides a holistic and accessible understanding of a covenant, defined as more than a contract, but critically, a spiritual oath signifying a divine commitment in a manner that richly informs an eclectic group of stakeholders within and even beyond the Church.

From the inside, this book provides not only a historical grounding of the Covenant but also something of a handbook that guides the lives of parishioners tasked with adhering to its fundamental tenets. Beyond the walls of the Church, this book serves as a powerful signal about its principles that helps clarify the indispensable role of the Church from both a religious, spiritual, and communal perspective. It is the communal perspective that readers will find most fascinating and inspirational for what it reaffirms about how the covenant cannot be fully realized in absence of supporting the overall well-being of communities in which the Church is situated.

Among the book's many strengths is how Dr. Hanson draws upon historical context, personal experiences, and a signature commitment to biblical explication to establish a deep understanding of the Covenant. When readers engage this text, they will develop a deep historically grounded view of the Covenant and how it is manifested in the day-to-day work of being a parishioner both in theory and practice. The historical references emerge as an important foundational aspect of Dr. Hanson's discussion because it signals his unwavering commitment to and belief in the continued relevance of the Covenant and its implications for the contemporary Church. In classic Black preacher exegesis, Dr. Hanson's discussion of the Covenant, in all its dimensions, is grounded in a deep, sophisticated understanding of scripture frequently referenced throughout the book. Those most familiar with Dr. Hanson's preaching style, and that which defines the Black Church more generally, will find his writing quite familiar. But even those unfamiliar will find his nuanced discussion not merely convincing and substantive but also accessible.

This is an important book that provides a necessary and timely road map for any Black Baptist Church that seeks to recapture a doctrinal view of the Covenant in the service of ensuring religious and spiritual efficacy but also maximizing the Church's impact on its community.

- **Dr. Gregory D. Wilson**
  The Ohio State University
  Ohio, USA

INTRODUCTION

"Church Covenant" written by John Newton Brown, Published in the Baptist Church Manual of 1853 states:

"Having been led, as we believe by the Spirit of God, to receive the Lord Jesus Christ as our Savior and, on the profession of our faith, having been baptized in the name of the Father, and of the Son, and of the Holy Spirit, we do now, in the presence of God, and this assembly, most solemnly and joyfully enter into covenant with one another as one body in Christ. We engage, therefore, by the aid of the Holy Spirit to walk together in Christian love; to strive for the advancement of this church, in knowledge, holiness, and comfort; to promote its prosperity and spirituality and to sustain its worship, ordinances, discipline, and doctrines; to contribute cheerfully and regularly to the support of the ministry, the expenses of the church, the relief of the poor, and the spread of the gospel through all nations. We also engage to maintain family and secret devotions; to religiously educate our children; to seek the salvation of our kindred and acquaintances; to walk circumspectly in the world; to be just in our dealings, faithful in our engagements, and exemplary in our deportment; to avoid all tattling, backbiting, and excessive anger; to abstain from the sale of, and use of, intoxicating drinks as a beverage; to be zealous in our efforts to advance the kingdom of our Savior. We further engage to watch over one another in brotherly love; to remember one another in prayer; to aid one another in sickness and distress; to cultivate Christian sympathy in feeling and Christian courtesy in speech; to be slow to take offense, but always

ready for reconciliation and mindful of the rules of our Savior to secure it without delay. We moreover engage that when we remove from this place we will, as soon as possible, unite with some other church where we can carry out the spirit of this covenant and the principles of God's Word."

"Reverend's Reflections: A Covenant Journey"

Within the sacred walls of United Faith Missionary Baptist Church, the air is still vibrant with the resonance of worship. Sundays there transcended mere routine, becoming a harmonious blend of devotion and long-standing tradition. It was here, under the wise leadership of Reverend Dr. Reginald Haywood, that I first entered into a legacy of faith that profoundly shaped my path.

First Sundays held a special place, a holy refuge where African American Baptists gathered in solemn duty and deep respect. The morning light poured through the stained glass, bathing the sanctuary as I soaked in the comforting rituals: the powerful delivery of the pastor, the communion table arrayed in white, and the deacons' reverent procession, their hands covered in white gloves.

These rituals became cherished memories that ignited my spiritual zeal. As a child, I recreated these scenes, instilling my play with the gravity I observed. Little did I understand then how these vibrant experiences were molding my future.

Years later, as the pastor of the New Nazareth Missionary Baptist Church, a deeper calling awakened in me—a desire to explore and rejuvenate the covenant that steered my spiritual journey. Moving beyond simple nostalgia, I embarked on an exploration to uncover the scriptural foundations of our covenant, revitalizing its age-old values.

In this book, I offer not only insight but also passion—a deep-seated eagerness to shed light on the sacred truths at the heart of our covenantal bonds. I invite fellow pastors, clergy, and all believers to embark with me on this path of enlightenment, to challenge misconceptions and grasp the profound depths of our collective faith.

Let this book serve not merely as an academic work but as a source of inspiration, nurturing growth and commitment within Baptist communities everywhere. Together, we will renew our covenantal commitments, drawing on the enduring strength of our faith.

Within the pages of this book, you will discover far more than mere historical reflections. You will find a road map to a future grounded in the enduring principles drawn from God's Word. Throughout these chapters, you will notice my frequent use of the term "covenant." It is essential to understand that while our "Church Covenant" is deeply influenced by Scripture, it does not supersede the authority of the Bible. Rather, it serves to enrich and supplement our faith, anchoring our community's beliefs and practices firmly within the framework of sacred Scripture.

1

What Is a Covenant?

In the tapestry of divine interaction woven throughout Scripture, the concept of a covenant stands as a profound thread binding the narrative of God's enduring relationship with humanity. A covenant, in its most sacred form, is not merely a contract or a promise—it is a divine oath whereby one party, typically one that is superior, pledges to bless or serve another, often in a specified manner. This pledge may be conditional, hinging on the fidelity of the recipient, or it may be given as an unconditional gift, a testament to grace and sovereign will.

The Hebrew term *berit*, translating directly as "covenant," carries with it the weight of being bound together. Derived from *bara*, meaning "to bind," it suggests not just a binding but a forging of relationships that holds the participants to their highest commitments. The New Testament adopts the Greek term *diatheke*, emphasizing the nature of the divine promise—not as a mutual agreement (*suntheke*) but as an oath, a one-sided commitment that God initiates and fulfills based on His gracious character.

In the biblical context, human covenants often mirrored social or political treaties—agreements crafted between equals or between a sovereign and a vassal. However, divine covenants transcend these earthly models, presenting a picture where the Almighty binds Himself to His creation in a display of inexplicable love and mercy. These divine covenants frame the structure of biblical revelation, demarcating it into what we refer to as the Old and New Testaments, each a testament to God's unfolding plan of redemption.

As we ponder the covenants detailed in Scripture—from the promises made to Abraham, to the laws given to Moses, and the New Covenant inaugurated through Christ—we see a pattern of profound commitment that God initiates and sustains. Each covenant builds upon the previous, revealing more of God's nature and His intentions for humanity.

In our own lives, understanding the nature of divine covenants invites us to reflect on the reliability of God's promises. It challenges us to consider our responses to His commitments. Are we like the Israelites, prone to wander and forget, or do we hold steadfast, trusting in the promises made to us through Christ?

Furthermore, recognizing the nature of God's covenantal promises should transform how we engage with others. Just as God's pledges are not flimsy agreements but solemn vows, so too should our words and commitments reflect integrity and intentionality. In a world where promises are often broken and commitments lightly made, adopting a covenantal approach to our relationships can offer a witness to the binding truth of God's unchanging faithfulness.

Thus, the covenant is not just a theological concept to be studied; it is a reality to be lived. In it, we find the assurance that God is bound to us with a promise that He will never break. And in this divine assurance, we find the courage to live out our commitments to God and to each other with a fidelity that mirrors His own. This is the profound legacy of the covenant—not just written on scrolls and pages, but inscribed on the hearts of those who believe.

A Church Covenant is a profound declaration, a commitment not only to God but also to a local congregation and to one's own self. It serves as a vivid encapsulation of our collective way of life, transcending even the detailed articulations of faith statements. While it may not enumerate every command on obedience, it beautifully outlines the ethos of living as a follower of Christ.

The Baptist Church Covenant is essentially a personal vow made in the presence of God, affirming one's dedication to His (Jesus') church and its mission. It represents a moral declaration, wherein, as historian Charles W. DeWeese articulates, it consists of "a series of written pledges based on the Bible which church members voluntarily make to God and to one another regarding their basic moral and spiritual commitments and the practice of their faith" (*Baptist Church Covenants*, p. viii). It is what one theologian describes as the "ethical counterpart to confessions of faith."

The practical application of a Church Covenant stretches across every facet of life, offering a Christian perspective that molds our daily actions and interactions. It emphasizes that membership within the church is not a passive commitment but an active engagement in living out faith based upon a shared understanding of Scripture.

Grounded in biblical principles, a Church Covenant is especially pivotal in congregations that uphold Biblical church discipline. It encourages members to exhort one another towards holiness and confront, with compassion and conviction, any persistent sin within the community. Thus, a Church Covenant is not just a set of ideals; it is a dynamic, living guide that shapes the character and conduct of a church and its members, urging them towards a more devout and disciplined spiritual life.

2

The Origin of the Covenant

In the mid-19th century, amid the growing complexity of American religious life, John Newton Brown emerged as a pivotal figure in the Baptist tradition. As a pastor and publisher, Brown was deeply committed to the edification of church members through a structured understanding of faith and practice. His seminal work, *The Baptist Church Manual*, published in 1853, remains a cornerstone in the Baptist educational corpus. With over a million copies printed to date, this manual not only guides new and prospective members through the nuances of Baptist belief and practice, but it also anchors them in the responsibilities inherent to membership in a local congregation.

The heart of Brown's manual is twofold: it includes both the "New Hampshire Confession of Faith" and a meticulously drafted church covenant. The New Hampshire Confession, crafted around 1833, was adopted by the New Hampshire Convention and has since been embraced by Baptists predominantly in the Northern and Western States. It is celebrated for articulating Baptist doctrines not with stern rigidity but in a tone that resonates with the compassion and mildness of the faith's deeper virtues.

Marshal Davis, reflecting on Baptist documents, articulates that they primarily serve two functions. The first, such as the Baptist Confession of Faith, delineates the doctrinal landscape of our belief system—what might be considered the theological backbone of the Baptist faith. The second, the Church Covenant, ventures into the practical arena, guiding the daily walk and mutual accountability of church members. Here, orthodoxy (right belief) and orthopraxy (right practice) intertwine, revealing the full spectrum of spiritual life as envisaged by Baptist theology.

This duality mirrors the apostle Paul's approach in his epistles, notably in Ephesians, where the first half lays a theological foundation (Ephesians 1–3), and the second addresses ethical living (Ephesians 4–6). Paul's writings exemplify how doctrinal truths are inseparable from the ethical duties they engender; belief is always in service to practice. This structure underlines a critical message: doctrine inherently carries the responsibility of duty. Every theological precept is designed not merely to inform but to transform, cultivating a life of Christian deportment that reflects the teachings of Christ.

3

Why the Covenant?

The Covenant serves as a profound affirmation of the identity bestowed upon us by God. It binds us as a community of believers, not through mere agreement, but through a divine pact made in the presence of God and under the guidance of the Holy Spirit. This covenant underscores our existence under a theocracy, where we are governed not by secular laws or democratic processes, but by divine decree. Our mission is to adhere faithfully to the commands of God's Word, ensuring that our worship, witness, and work not only glorify God but also carry the message of salvation to the unsaved.

The necessity of the Covenant lies in the structure it provides—offering clear guidelines and boundaries for our spiritual conduct. It reminds us that our relationship with God and each other within the church is based upon covenantal, not contractual, terms. A prevailing challenge within the faith community is the misconception that we can negotiate with God. However, there is no bargaining with the Divine; God remains unchanging in His essence and His Word, irrespective of our personal or cultural contexts. The Bible firmly states, "Because it is written, Be ye holy; for I am holy," highlighting the expectation that we rise to meet God's standards. Achieving this requires complete submission to the mandates of His Word.

To live a life truly aligned with the teachings of Christ requires a deep, unwavering commitment—a complete submission to the mandates of His Word. This profound dedication forms the cornerstone of our Church Covenant, a sacred agreement that binds us not only to God but to each other, in a shared journey of faith and fidelity. As we explore the pillars of this covenant, we uncover the ways in which it molds our community's identity, enhances our spiritual discipline, and amplifies our witness to the world. These are not just ideals; they are practical actions and commitments that forge a distinctive path for every believer.

1. **Community Identity and Commitment:** Embracing the Covenant within the church encourages a shared identity and collective commitment to live out God's commands. It fortifies the community's unity and purpose, making the church a distinct body that operates on divine principles rather than human ones.

2. **Holiness and Submission:** The call to holiness is a central theme of the Covenant. It challenges individuals and congregations alike to pursue a life of purity and devotion, aligned with God's expectations rather than societal norms. This pursuit must be marked by a willing submission to God's directives, acknowledging that true transformation requires divine intervention and guidance.

3. **Witness and Evangelism:** By living according to the Covenant, believers are positioned to effectively witness to non-believers. The integrity and distinctiveness of a life lived under God's commands can serve as a powerful testament to His grace and truth, drawing others towards salvation.

4. **Spiritual Discipline:** The Covenant provides a framework for spiritual discipline, guiding believers in their daily decisions and interactions. It calls for a regular examination of one's life and adjustments in accordance with God's Word, promoting continual spiritual growth and maturity.

By adhering to the Covenant, believers affirm their identity as God's chosen people and accept the responsibility to live distinctively under His sovereign rule. This commitment not only deepens personal faith but also strengthens the communal witness of the church, offering a beacon of divine truth in a world governed by secular values.

4

The Foundation of the Covenant

The Foundation of Our Covenant is subsumed under Christ's atoning effort. *"Having been led, as we believe, by the Spirit of God, to receive the Lord Jesus Christ as our Savior, and on the profession of our faith, having been baptized in the name of the Father, and of the Son, and of the Holy Ghost."*

This requirement serves several important functions. Firstly, it underscores the notion that true communion with the church body is grounded in a personal relationship with Christ. This relationship is initiated by divine intervention—specifically the guidance of the Holy Spirit—who leads an individual to acknowledge Jesus Christ, not merely as a historical figure or a prophet, but as the personal Savior who redeems from sin. The eligibility for participation in church covenants being tied to these spiritual milestones emphasizes the seriousness with which personal faith is treated within Baptist circles.

This framework ensures that those entering into covenant relationships within the church are not only affirming a set of beliefs intellectually, but they are also experiencing and living out these truths in a transformative, personal ideal of Jesus as both Lord and Savior. This is crucial. It implies not only a rescue from sin by Jesus the Savior, but it also implies an ongoing daily authority over one's life by submitting to Jesus the Lord. This dual role of Christ impacts how believers conduct themselves, both within the church and in broader society. The personal faith in Christ as Lord and Savior not only forms the bedrock of individual spiritual life, but it also fundamentally shapes the communal life of the church.

In essence, the church covenant is not a mere formality but a sacred bond that reflects the inner spiritual reality of each member. It highlights a collective journey of faith, rooted in individual commitments to Christ, and reinforced by the shared experiences of baptism and spiritual guidance. This foundational approach ensures that the church is built not just on common beliefs but on genuinely transformed lives.

A. The Commencement—Having Been Led

"For as many as are led by the Spirit of God, they are the sons of God" [1] (Romans 8:14). What does it mean to be led? The word "led" is translated in the Greek as, "ago"; it means, "to so influence others as to cause them to follow a recommended course of action, to guide, to direct" [2]. The Holy Spirit, in His guiding role, steers us toward the restorative flow emanating from the Cross's base.

How does this guidance manifest? Interestingly, "led" also connotes being taken into custody or arrested, illustrating the Holy Spirit's method of guidance. Through the proclamation of the Gospel, the Spirit seizes us, bringing our sins and faults to light, thereby compelling us to recognize our need for the Savior.

This relationship is not one of us wielding control over the Spirit; rather, it is the Spirit who wields control, making us instruments of Divine Will. As we enter into a covenant, it is the Holy Spirit who navigates our course, drawing us into profound communion through His divine orchestration.

I have been personally influenced and seized by this force. Resistance to such guidance, which I liken to spiritual terrorism, involves rejecting the Spirit's authority and refusing to be captivated by His direction.

The persistent and ongoing nature of this guidance, as suggested by the present tense of "led," calls us to continually reside under the Holy Spirit's watchful care. This is not merely a transient commitment but a lifelong one, where justification leads to sanctification. God desires not only to be our Savior, but He also desires to be our sovereign Lord, exerting full control over our lives. While many may accept His salvation, they often hesitate to trust Him for guidance across all life aspects. God's intention is not merely to lease us for a time; He aims to possess us completely, reflecting His total ownership and our complete surrender to His will.

B. The Creed—As We Believe

Our beliefs are clearly articulated within the framework of the Covenant. One might wonder why would anyone commit to a covenant or agreement laden with doctrinal uncertainties? Indeed, a lack of faith in the foundational creed jeopardizes one's ability to faithfully uphold the covenant's terms. So, what is it that we hold to be true? We affirm the all-encompassing work of the Cross accomplished through Jesus Christ, alone. Through Him, we are redeemed, reconciled, regenerated, and promised resurrection or rapture as stated in John 3:16.

The term "believe" refers to a trustful human response to God's self-revelation through His words and deeds. My belief in God is anchored in His WORD and His WONDERS. God has made Himself known through His Word and has substantiated it through His wonders. The Cross and Crucifixion, prophesied in Scripture, were actualized in the miraculous event of Him conquering the grave. The enduring emptiness of the grave stands as a testament to the reliability of His Word and fortifies my faith.

Exploring the Greek nuances of belief ("pistis" and "peitho") are particularly significant. "Pistis" denotes a belief in the truth, reality, or doctrine—the established articles of faith. "Peitho" suggests a persuasion that guides one's confidence and commitment, often leading to a changed viewpoint or action based on revealed truth.

These convictions about Christ not only fuel our beliefs, but they also reinforce our commitment to the covenant. This brings to mind a phrase often used by seasoned believers: "You can't make me doubt Him, because I know too much about Him." The redemptive work of triumph over death compels me to believe. Should our faith waver or become clouded by doubts? We need only remind ourselves of the Gospel's power. If Christ has indeed conquered the grave, then surely He can master any of our trials.

C. The Comforter—By the Spirit of God.

R. A. Torrey says, "Before one can correctly understand the work of the Holy Spirit, he must first of all, know the Spirit Himself. A frequent source of error and fanaticism about the work of the Holy Spirit is the attempt to study and understand His work without coming to know Him as a person [3]. This statement, both profoundly accurate and deeply unfortunate, reveals a troubling reality: many within our congregations are unfamiliar with the true nature of the Holy Spirit, having relegated Him to merely a source of emotional highs and euphoric experiences. This misconception is not trivial; it is essential to the very vitality and health of both the church and its members.

The Holy Spirit is not merely an emotion or a fleeting sensation. He is not an ephemeral force we can "catch" or experience in sporadic bursts. Nor is He a person who merely brushes against us momentarily. When we perceive the Holy Spirit merely as just a feeling or a sensation, our focus tends to be self-serving by interrogating, i.e., "How can I get more of the Holy Spirit?" This perspective leads us to view Him as a resource to be utilized rather than a person to be known and loved.

Conversely, when we understand Him as the Bible portrays—a Divine Person with a will, emotions, and intellect, our approach shifts fundamentally. Instead of seeking to control or harness Him, we begin to ask, "How can the Holy Spirit have more of me?" This question invites a deeper relationship, one of which we are led by Him and continually surrender ourselves to His guidance and governance. This shift is crucial for anyone seeking a genuine, transformative engagement with the Holy Spirit, forming the cornerstone of a life truly led by God.

In the Old Testament, the Holy Spirit is described as "rûaḥ," a feminine noun that translates spirit, wind, or *breath,* and refers to the Spirit of God or the Lord. The Spirit of God was the source of inspiration for prophets, providing prophetic declarations and empowering those called to serve.

In the New Testament, the term used is "pneúma," which also means, "breath." Here, the Holy Spirit takes on roles of illumination and empowerment for Christians, offering spiritual knowledge, aid, consolation, sanctification, and intercession.

These definitions highlight the indispensable role of the Holy Spirit in the life of the church and the believer. It is through the agency of the Holy Ghost that we are revitalized, invigorated, and brought to life. Without His presence, we lack the ability to exercise spiritual gifts or gain insights into His Word. Every believer should cherish the Holy Ghost, for it is through Him that we maintain our connection with heaven and find guidance through the challenges of life. His role is not just supportive but foundational, enabling us to navigate life's adversities with divine insight and strength.

D. The Christos—To Receive the Lord Jesus Christ As our Savior

By virtue of Jesus Christ's redemptive sacrifice, we gain entry into both the covenant and the family of faith. What, then, has He saved us from? Christ rescues us from sin's presence, power, and penalty, delivering us from its all-encompassing grasp. The term "savior" encompasses the acts of delivering, preserving, healing, and providing. Jesus embodied these roles on Earth as our High Priest, Prophet, and King, fulfilling scriptural prophecies. Through Him, we are elevated to being joint heirs with Christ, entitled to a profound inheritance, for He is both our regal and prophetic fulfillment.

Every believer should be profoundly thankful for this salvation. As members of this covenant, we are assured and insured by the knowledge that God cares for those He has redeemed. The blessings we receive are immensely greater than we deserve, accessible through our inclusion in this covenant. Salvation itself represents liberation from danger and suffering, with the term "to rescue" implying not just escape but ongoing protection.

The reality of sin subjects every individual to the mortal penalty of death, a sentence we are powerless to annul on our own. Only through deliverance, necessitating Jesus' incarnation, can we be freed. Thus, Jesus, the Son of Man, came to seek and save the lost (Luke 19:10), fulfilling the essential need for salvation and embodying the ultimate act of divine rescue.

E. The Command—Baptizing Them

The Christian rite of initiation is practiced by almost all who profess to embrace the Christian faith. In the New Testament era, persons professing Christ were immersed in water as a public confession of their faith in Jesus the Savior. This was accomplished in direct obedience to the explicit mandate of the Lord (Matthew 28:16–20)[4]. Baptism represents the death, burial, and resurrection of our Lord and Savior Jesus the Christ. We approach the liquid grave submerging the old man and coming up a new person. The token of baptism is given to those who have accepted Jesus as Lord and have accepted His teachings.

The word "baptism" comes from the word "*baptizō*"; fut. *baptísō*, from *báptō* (911), to dip; immerse, submerge for a religious purpose, to overwhelm, saturate, baptize"[5]. The activity of baptism was revealed to us by John the Baptist in Matthew Chapter 3, "Then went out to him Jerusalem, and all Judaea, and all the region round about Jordan, 6 And were baptized of him in Jordan, confessing their sins" [6] (Matthew 3:6). John utilized baptism as a religious ritual.

John's message was one of rebuke and warning. He called for people to repent before the "coming" of the Lord. People responded to his preaching and were baptized. Baptism, or ritual immersion as the Jews described it, was frequent in Israel. Jewish people immersed themselves in ritual baths before entering the holy place as a sign of inner purification. The Jewish sect of the Essenes in the desert at Qumran used ritual baths frequently to represent ritual purification. Converts to Judaism also would undergo such a ritual as part of their initiation into the faith.

So, "baptism," as the Gospels call it, was fairly common in the religious life of Israel. John, though, was pressing them with an urgency to repent before it was too late: "The ax is already at the root of the trees, and every tree that does not produce good fruit will be cut down and thrown into the fire." It was a warning for people to repent; and repentance meant a change of life, not just feeling sorry for wrongs done.

Jesus came to be baptized not because He was a sinner or for confession, but Jesus said that He *must* be baptized "to fulfill all righteousness" [7] (Matthew 3:15). Jesus was baptized to be identified with the sinner. Isaiah says, it was "because He poured out His life unto death, and was numbered with the transgressors. For He bore the sin of many, and made intercession for the transgressors" [8].

F. The Criteria

"In the name of the Father, and of the Son and of the Holy Ghost." Baptism in this manner signifies our profound identification with the Trinity. By being baptized, we declare our allegiance to the Father, celebrate our salvation through the Son, and acknowledge the indwelling of the Holy Spirit. This act mirrors the authority by which we invoke Jesus' name in prayer, as outlined in John 14:13, where praying in Jesus' name means appealing to God the Father with the authority of His Son.

Jesus explicitly commands baptism "in the name of the Father, of the Son, and of the Holy Spirit" (Matthew 28:19). Thus this underlines a triune identification that marks our lives with their divine authority and presence. This directive is part of what is famously known as, "The Great Commission," where the resurrected Christ instructs His disciples to disseminate His teachings globally and to consolidate followers' commitment through baptism.

Controversies regarding the correct baptismal formula persist today, with debates centering on whether to baptize "in the Name of the Father, and of the Son, and of the Holy Ghost" or "in the Name of Jesus." Understanding the scriptural context is crucial to resolving this. In Acts 2:38, Peter's response to the convicted crowd—"Repent, and be baptized every one of you in the name of Jesus Christ for the remission of sins, and ye shall receive the gift of the Holy Ghost"—addresses a specific inquiry, not establishing a new liturgical formula. Peter was not amending the commission but fulfilling it, as Jesus had already established the baptismal formula during His Great Commission.

As Baptists, we adhere to the Trinitarian formula not only because it aligns us with the theological roles of the Father, Son, and Holy Spirit—the Progenitor, the Propitiation, and the Paraclete—but because it follows the mandate given by Christ Himself. We hold no authority to alter what Christ has prescribed. The integrity of Peter's ministry underscores this; he faithfully executed Christ's commands without deviation.

Thus, in our practices and teachings, we must maintain fidelity to the commission as Christ authorized it, recognizing that our role is not to reinterpret or modify divine instructions, but to obey and implement them faithfully.

G. The Communion—We Do Now in the Presence of God and This Assembly

We, the people of the covenant, first and foremost, pledge our loyalty and commitment to Him who has brought us into the fellowship of Christ's Body. The ecclesia has a primary duty to the Father. The moment of conversion and the subsequent symbol of immersion are public declarations to the church of our willingness to submit to God's sovereign rule and our commitment to please God alone via the faithful performance of that which He has prescribed.

It must forever be engraved in our minds that even though we do not have a corporeal representation of God in our presence, our commitment to him and our accountability to the covenant is still grave and solemn. God is *Wise, Omniscient, Omnipotent,* and *Providential,* and I believe that, at times, we as saints can forget this and become lethargic when it comes to our end of the covenant.

The Bible says, "Behold, He that keepeth Israel shall neither slumber nor sleep" [9]. God doesn't become lax, lazy, or lethargic when it comes to His job. He is faithful and alert. He is ever ready to fulfill what He said He will do. "God *is* our refuge and strength, a very present help in trouble" [10].

Yes, difficulties arise; yes, trials and tribulations raise their hands to buffet us; but our love for God and our covenant with Him and His church should not let us waver in our commitment to honoring that promise. Our covenant states that we not only affirm this in the presence of God, but it also affirms in the presence of the assembly. Salvation initiates us into the covenant baptism which signifies our acceptance of the covenant, but our continued communion and participation in the "Last Supper" is what sustains and renews our commitment. This part of the covenant makes us accountable to the pastor and the church and her governance, rules, and regulations.

I've found that most individuals are fine with being responsible to God, but they bristle at the idea of being responsible to their pastor and their church. Does the Bible teach church accountability? Let's see what Jesus has to say about that: "Moreover if thy brother shall trespass against thee, go and tell him his fault between thee and him alone: if he shall hear thee, thou hast gained thy brother. [16] But if he will not hear *thee, then* take with thee one or two more, that in the mouth of two or three witnesses every word may be established. [17] And if he shall neglect to hear them, tell *it* unto the church: but if he neglect to hear the church, let him be unto thee as an heathen man and a publican" [11] Matthew 18:15-17. Our Lord Jesus Christ teaches us this principle to remind us that pastors and churches have the authority from God to maintain scriptural guidelines by which believers are to live and conduct themselves.

In the Book of Acts, the apostle Peter had a similar situation that necessitated this instance of church accountability. Acts 5:1-11 says, "But a certain man named Ananias, with Sapphira his wife, sold a possession, [2] And kept back *part* of the price, his wife also being privy *to it*, and brought a certain part, and laid *it* at the apostles' feet. [3] But Peter said, Ananias, 'Why hath Satan filled thine heart to lie to the Holy Ghost, and to keep back *part* of the price of the land? [4] While it remained, was it not thine own? And after it was sold, was it not in thine own power? Why hast thou conceived this thing in thine heart? Thou hast not lied unto men, but unto God.' [5] And Ananias hearing these words fell down, and gave up the ghost: And great fear came on all them that heard these things. [6] And the young men arose, wound him up, and carried *him* out, and buried *him*. [7] And it was about the space of three hours after, when his wife, not knowing what was done, came in. [8] And Peter answered unto her, 'Tell me whether ye sold the land for so much?' And she said, 'Yea, for so much.' [9] Then Peter said unto her, 'How is it that ye have agreed together to tempt the Spirit of the Lord? Behold, the feet of them which have buried thy husband *are* at the door, and shall carry thee out.' [10] Then fell she down straightway at his feet, and yielded up the ghost: and the young men came in, and found her dead, and, carrying *her* forth, buried *her* by her husband. [11] And great fear came upon all the church, and upon as many as heard these things" [12] .

God expects us to be mindful of our covenant with Him, but He also expects us to do the same with each other. By submitting to the covenant, we are making an affirmation that we will follow the pastor and fulfill our responsibilities to our church and the brothers and sisters in the faith.

Not only is it important for us to remember our covenant with God but also with one another. By committing ourselves to the terms of the covenant, we are stating unequivocally that we will follow the pastor and live up to the commitments we have made to both our local church and the other believers who share our faith.

H. The Celebration—Most Solemnly and Joyfully Enter into Covenant with One Another as One Body in Christ.

The Bible says: "Make a joyful noise to the Lord, all the earth! ² Serve the Lord with gladness! Come into his presence with singing! ³ Know that the Lord, he is God! It is he who made us, and we are his; we are his people, and the sheep of his pasture. ⁴ Enter his gates with thanksgiving, and his courts with praise! Give thanks to him; bless his name! ⁵ For the Lord is good; his steadfast love endures forever, and his faithfulness to all generations" [13] (Psalm 100).

The Psalm we often turn to in moments of praise and worship reveals not only the call to worship, but it also profoundly illustrates the "how" of our devotion and labor. The Psalmist enjoins us to "serve Him with gladness," a directive that shines a light on the joy and pleasure inherent in our covenant with God.

Imagine the profound relationship we are invited into: to be in covenant with the Creator of the universe, the One who orchestrated "creation ex-nihilo." He who crafted the cosmos with splendor, who scattered stars across the velvet night, and adorned our world with the sun and moon-like celestial medallions, who calls us to a partnership of joy that is unparalleled by any earthly agreement.

Why then would any believer serve such a magnificent God with anything less than a full heart? Why would we approach this divine relationship with downcast eyes or a spirit of reluctance? Each moment of service to God should be met with readiness and jubilation, a celebration of the privilege to work in His name.

Yet, entering this joyous covenant also bears a solemn responsibility. Solemnity here does not imply a lack of joy; rather, it insists that our duties under the covenant be approached with wholehearted sincerity. What value is there in service rendered with a spirit that is only half-engaged? "This people draweth nigh unto me with their mouth, and honoureth me with their lips; but their heart is far from me. But in vain they do worship me, teaching for doctrines the commandments of men."

Our joy in our relationship with the progenitor of the covenant should ignite a fervor to give our utmost in service. Solemnity and joyfulness are not mutually exclusive but intertwined, reminding us that sincerity and exuberance must coalesce in our labors for the Lord.

5

The Functionalities of the Covenant

I. The Assistance Needed to Function within the Covenant

We engage by the Aid of the Holy Spirit.

Since the covenant lays the groundwork for us to put our beliefs into practice, it motivates us to think and act in accordance with its teachings. The doctrine should be followed by the obligation, and all information should result in the implementation of the doctrine.

I am aware that these ideas pertaining to the covenant are exceedingly Utopian and appear to be impossible to put into practice. With that being said, the challenge now is figuring out how to complete the assignments we've been given. We engage only by and through the aid and assistance of the Holy Spirit. We need the assistance and presence of the Holy Spirit our Paraclete, Advocate, and Comforter.

The Greek word is "parakletos"; from the verb parakaleo. The word for "Paraclete" is passive in form, and etymologically signifies "called to one's side" [14]. This word is also defined as one who is a helper, and since it is in the present tense, it denotes that the Holy Spirit is continuously and constantly helping us.

Without the consistent assistance of the Holy Spirit, neither our life in Christ nor our desire to fulfill these tasks within the church can be attained to the level we would like. I am of the opinion that the peril we are witnessing in the world at this time is the sickness of our churches and the saints who are endeavoring to minister apart from the support of the Master. We are always in need of His help and assistance, and if He is not present in our ministries, we are nothing more than receptacles holding content that will eventually spoil and rot because we do not have the means to distribute it.

It is possible to be gifted, talented, learned, full of perception, and well-instructed; yet, if we do not have the approval of the Holy Spirit, none of these things will be of any use to us or God. I am thankful that not only is He by our side, but He also lives within us: "And I will pray the Father, and He shall give you another Comforter, that He may abide with you for ever; [17] *Even* the Spirit of truth; whom the world cannot receive, because it seeth Him not, neither knoweth Him: but ye know Him; for He dwelleth with you, and shall be in you. [18] I will not leave you comfortless: I will come to you" (John 14:16-18) [15].

II. The Activity of the Saint within the Covenant

To Walk Together in Christian Love

The two words "walk" and love" need to be highlighted in this section of study. They are both in the active voice. This suggests that these two activities must be performed and initiated by the saints. Paul tells the church in Galatia to "Walk in the Spirit" Galatians 5:16 [16]. John instructs the church in 1 John 4:7 by saying, "Beloved, let us love one another" [17]. The word "walk" comes from the Greek word "peripateo," which means, to live or to conduct one's life in an orderly manner.

The word love ("Agapeo") means to esteem or to regard with strong affection. The idea of walking together in Christian love suggests that believers should have a vested interested in the spiritual welfare of one another. Our Christian connection is evidenced by the love we have one for another. Our love is seen through our conduct and how we treat one another.

In the Bible, there is no mandate to like anyone, but it does tell us to love, and our love is a by-product of our relationship with Christ. Love reveals our salvific claim, the apostle John says that "We know that we have passed from death unto life, because we love the brethren. He that loveth not *his* brother abideth in death" (1 John 3:14) [18].

Because of my love for Christ, I am able to walk in faith with the family of God; anyone who refuses to do so, on the other hand, reveals their disdain for their brother and takes joy in dwelling among the dead. The problem we face in the church is that there are members who refuse to walk in accordance with the vision and voice of the pastor. This is due to the fact that there are loveless saints in the congregation who do not have a pulse or a heartbeat for the work that is being done in the ministry. Their hatred is revealed by their disconnection and disdain for everyone and everything. They are the first to complain and the last to contribute. My experience has shown me that it is impossible to coerce individuals into doing things they do not love; however, it is important to keep in mind that if there is no love there is no life, that ultimately deems them as ecclesiastical corpses.

III. The Assimilation

To Strive for the Advancement of This Church

What is the church striving for? Where is our effort guiding us, and how do we strive for the advancement of the church?

A. Knowledge

A working definition of knowledge is, "The truth or facts of life that a person acquires either through experience or thought" [19]. Knowledge consists of having a better understanding of God's will in an ethical sense. Paul says, "For this cause we also, since the day we heard *it*, do not cease to pray for you, and to desire that ye might be filled with the knowledge of His will in all wisdom and spiritual understanding; [10] That ye might walk worthy of the Lord unto all pleasing, being fruitful in every good work, and increasing in the knowledge of God [20] (Col. 1:9-10).

The more we strive to know about God, the more our lives are transformed for the sake of His glory. Christian Education should be at the forefront of every church. Every Christian should desire to know more about Him, not for the sake of arrogance and conceit, but for the purposes of alteration and apologetics.

B. Holiness

Holiness has to do primarily with "God's separating from the world that which He chooses to devote to Himself" [21]. "Having therefore these promises, dearly beloved, let us cleanse ourselves from all filthiness of the flesh and spirit, perfecting holiness in the fear of God" [22] (1 Corinthians 7:1).

Holiness affects us in a moral and an ethical sense that changes our behavior. We must strive to be holy. It must be our sincere desire to change our deportment and or lives. This goal cannot be accomplished with ascetic practices; rather, we must rely exclusively on the miraculous strength of the Holy Spirit to accomplish it.

C. Comfort

1 Thessalonians 4:18 says, "Wherefore comfort one another with these words" [23]. Paul is admonishing the church to encourage one

another and to edify the saints. As is common knowledge, life is full of challenges and obstacles, but the advantage of living in a community bound by a covenant is that we are encircled by a large cloud of witnesses who inspire faith and optimism in the face of adversity.

This is a blessing for a soul that has become weary. We owe a debt of gratitude to God for the testimonies of the saints, for in them, we discover a glimmer of hope hidden behind the gloom of every storm.

IV. The Advocacy

To Promote Its Prosperity and Spirituality

The entire covenant community must be concerned with the prosperity and spirituality of the church. The word "prosperity" is a word that has been perverted and debauched, which has caused the very essence of it to be misunderstood. The word "prosper" comes from the Greek word "**euodoo**"; eu-good, hodos-way or journey. The word suggests that one's journey would be well.

Everyone who is a part of the covenant has a responsibility to ensure that the church is well-maintained in every way, and it should be the aim of every member of the covenant to invest in the prosperity of the church or the covenant community. All of us, not just the pastor or deacons, are responsible for this.

In the New Testament Church, the people were so blessed by the fellowship that the bible says, "And all that believed were together, and had all things common; [45] And sold their possessions and goods, and parted them to all *men*, as every man had need. [46] And they, continuing daily with one accord in the temple, and breaking bread from house to house, did eat their meat with gladness and singleness of heart, [47] Praising God, and having favour with all the people. And the Lord added to the church daily such as should be saved" [24] (Acts 2:45-47). These believers cared deeply about the holistic health of the church. They showed their support not only by their presence, but also through financial contributions. They put a priority on spending time in fellowship!

The promotion of prosperity is also joined with spirituality, but what does spirituality really mean? Spirituality is a life lived within the structure defined by God's saving performances in His history with His people. God has outlined for us in His Word what it takes for us to be spiritual.

We must always remember that religion and spirituality are two different things. Religion is based on a set system of beliefs and regulations, but spirituality seeks to be wholly shaped by what we believe and are governed by, His sovereignty.

It is sad to say that some of our churches seek to be prosperous in materialism but yet remain unspiritual in the maintenance of His house. Isn't it strange that some people feel they are prosperous because of large churches, state of the art facilities, money, and fame, but yet they are a haven for iniquity and false doctrine? If you seek to be prosperous and have a well journey, seek to be spiritual! Listen to God's words to Joshua: "This book of the law shall not depart out of thy mouth; but thou shalt meditate therein day and night, that thou mayest observe to do according to all that is written therein: for then thou shalt make thy way prosperous, and then thou shalt have good success" [25] (Joshua 1:8).

V. The Aim

The word "sustain" means, to give support, to bear up under, to support the weight of: prop *also;* to carry or withstand (a weight or pressure) [26]. Worship, fulfilling Ordinances, Disciplines, and Doctrines, becomes a burden or responsibility for the church. Our support carries a great weight and responsibility which can not be done without sweat and struggle.

Some may ask, "Why are these components so cumbersome to carry out?" The answer to that question is this, the devil hates worship because it glorifies God. He hates Ordinances of the church because

Baptism solidifies new converts and Communion highlights salvation. He hates Discipline because it establishes order, and he hates Doctrine because it teaches us to refute that which is false and foolish. This is why we should feel the burden of sustaining and supporting these factors, they are vitally important to the Body of Christ (the Church).

A. Worship

"The term is used to refer to the act or action associated with attributing honor, reverence, or worth to that which is considered to be divine by religious adherents. Christian worship is often defined as the ascription of worth or honor to the triune God. Worship is more fully understood as an interrelation between divine action and human response: worship is the human response to the self-revelation of the triune God. This includes: (1) divine initiation in which God reveals Himself, His purposes, and His will; (2) a spiritual and personal relationship with God through Jesus Christ on the part of the worshiper; and (3) a response by the worshiper of adoration, humility, submission, and obedience to God" [27].

Worship is my personal appraisal of the divinity of God. It causes me to esteem and make a verbal assessment based on who He is and not just on what He does. Worship causes me to leave the trivial and focus on God, alone. Worship is not only our right, but it is a responsibility. When I am in his presence I have a saintly obligation to respond, I do not have a right to remain silent.

B. Ordinances

The ordinances of the Church are Baptism and Communion. The ordinance of Baptism places upon us the responsibility of engaging in evangelism and seeking to share the Gospel love message of Jesus Christ. This places upon us the greater burden to make sure that our baptisteries remain full and ready and not be turned into storage units for church furniture. New births should be a desire in the covenant community, and we must not lose sight on this important principle.

Communion is the way by which we renew our covenant vertical (with God our Father) and horizontally (with the saints of the covenant community, and we also show forth Jesus' death and suffering until He comes again. These things are important to the church and should not be taken lightly, no wonder the devil wishes to eradicate these two things. If there is no baptism, there is no new birth, and if the there is no communion, there is no fellowship with God or man. Satan has a desire to stop regeneration and fellowship, and it is ultimately because it is something Jesus instituted for His church. We must be sober and steadfast so that we can be able to defend what defines our faith and covenant.

C. Discipline

Discipline means, to train. "It usually refers in the Bible to moral training, which includes the positive aspect of instruction and the negative aspect of correction, sometimes punitive" [28]. The root word for discipline is disciple, and every disciple, after they have been taught, should have some moral training. If there is any assembly that should have moral training, it should be the covenant community/the church.

We are living in a time when people in our churches are shunning discipline. And it is simply because they view the church as a democracy and not a theocracy. Disciples should seek to be disciplined. Any person who tries to be non-submissive and non-compliant is not a disciple, but a diabolical vigilante who is motivated by self-interests to cause division within the Body of Christ.

D. Doctrine

Doctrine can be defined as "Christian truth and teaching passed on from generation to generation as the faith that was delivered to the saints [29]. Doctrine thus serves a vital and necessary role within the life of the church and the life of the believer. The biblical focus on doctrine is not based upon the notion of static and dead beliefs but upon living truths cherished and defended by all true Christians" [30].

Doctrine is the hinge on which the theology of the church swings. Our knowledge, ordinances, worship, and disciplines are based upon the Word of God, alone. There are those who will suggest that doctrine is traditional and non-spiritual, but I would say that to have no doctrine is to be non-spiritual. Ignorance is an enemy to the sanctity of the believer. Othodoxy leads to orthopraxy. When there is no doctrine, there is no duty. When there is poor doctrine, there is poor performance.

VI. The Allocation

To Contribute Cheerfully and Regularly

Our Covenant also admonishes us to be those who are willing and gracious to give of our substance. Paul admonished the church in Corinth to cheerfully give: "Every man according as he purposeth in his heart, *so let him give*; not grudgingly, or of necessity: for God loveth a cheerful giver" [31].

We should not only cheerfully give ,but we should also regularly give. This means, there are ought to be some consistency in our giving. Our giving should not be callous and inconsistent, but it should be done with joy and with the idea of knowing that service requires the resources of the community.

I am well aware that this subject is met with many views, judgments, and outlooks because many have allowed money to rule and regulate them, and the truth of the matter is that those who object to giving sometimes may be the ones who have become stingy with their resources. The Bible says, "For the love of money is the root of all evil: which while some coveted after, they have erred from the faith, and pierced themselves through with many sorrows" [32]. Why do we give?

1. The Support of the Ministry

Ministry requires services to the ministry that Jesus Christ commanded us to faithfully practice. Evangelism, Missions, Christian Education, Christian Development, and other elements that require time, gifts, and talent. Ministry requires money and resources.

2. The Expenses of the Church

Believe it or not, churches have bills! The building needs to be maintained. Lights and gas are necessities, and most of all, there can be no church without a pastor. As members of the Body of Christ, we have a covenant to make sure that the temple/church is to be maintained: "2 Thus speaketh the Lord of hosts, saying, This people say, The time is not come, the time that the Lord's house should be built.' 3 Then came the word of the Lord by Haggai the prophet, saying, 4 *Is it* time for you, O ye, to dwell in your cieled houses, And this house *lie* waste? 5 Now therefore thus saith the Lord of hosts; Consider your ways. 6 Ye have sown much, and bring in little; Ye eat, but ye have not enough; Ye drink, but ye are not filled with drink; Ye clothe you, but there is none warm; And he that earneth wages earneth wages *to put it* into a bag with holes" (Haggai 1:2-6) [33].

The maintenance of the church is also combined with the clerical care, "For it is written in the law of Moses, Thou shalt not muzzle the mouth of the ox that treadeth out the corn. Doth God take care for oxen? 10 Or saith he *it* altogether for our sakes? For our sakes, no doubt, *this* is written: that he that ploweth should plow in hope; and that he that thresheth in hope should be partaker of his hope" [34].

The church must have a vested interest in the welfare of the shepherd, and they must make sure that he has the resources necessary to execute effective ministry.

3. The Relief of the Poor

"Verily I say unto you, Inasmuch as ye have done *it* unto one of the least of these my brethren, ye have done *it* unto me" (Matthew 25:40) [35].

The community of faith has a great responsibility to the poor, especially to those who are a part of the household of faith, we must be aware that there are those, even in our churches who may not be as financially fortunate as others. So, our gifts that we regularly and cheerfully contribute should be present to aid assist.

4. The Spread of the Gospel to All Nations

The Gospel is bigger than a local address; it is a global reach. "Go ye therefore, and teach all nations, baptizing them in the name of the Father, and of the Son, and of the Holy Ghost: [20] Teaching them to observe all things whatsoever I have commanded you: and, lo, I am with you always, *even* unto the end of the world. Amen" (Matthew 28:19-20) [36].

This mission and mandate is what drives the ministry of the church. Our covenant arrests the hearts, hands, and minds of every congregant to engage in the work of moving the Gospel from the pew to the pavement. The church cannot drift into a recline because of the laurels we possess locally. Our evangelistic victories are only just the tip of the iceberg. We have a greater job to do and more work that encompasses us:

"Verily, verily, I say unto you, He that believeth on me, the works that I do shall he do also; and greater *works* than these shall he do; because I go unto my Father" [37].

The covenant reminds us to "spread" the Gospel. The idea of spreading the Gospel corresponds with the word "Go." The word "Go" in the Greek is *"poreúomai."* It refers to passing or passage, to pierce or run through. To transport oneself, to go from one place to another" [38]. The mandate to spread the Gospel requires that each church must be willing and ready to travel in order to transport this message of redemption. This little word "Go" causes us to reassess and reevaluate ministries as it relates to its mobility.

Have we really been *Missionary* Baptist churches? Or have we been *Stationary* Baptist churches? Our full service to the masses cannot be fully successful if we wish to only stay sequestered in the comfort our homes and sanctuaries. The Gospel isn't some magic powder we throw in the air and await for the shifting force of the wind to blow its particles into the areas of desired reform.

Those who are willing to travel into the rough and remote areas that have been forsaken, rejected, and ruled-out must transport the Gospel. The Gospel does so much for the disenfranchised. It reaches them right where they are. After all, that is what Jesus did for us! He left Glory and subjected Himself to the gruesomeness of this world, bore our guilt, and gave us the preciousness of grace.

What a mighty God we serve! He is a God who is always traveling to meet us right where we are. Surely we ought to be able to render the same unto others.

6

The Fundamentals of the Covenant

I. Maintain Devotions

Devotion is the activity that sets the tone for our day, for our life, and for the way we use our time, energy, and talents. It reveals that to which we are devoted, given, driven with a singleness of heart and determination of the mind" [39]. When we hear the word "devotion" for those of us who have been raised in the African American Baptist Church, the concept of devotion revolves around the deacons, who would position themselves at the front of the church and they would begin with a song, then a scripture, a Dr. Watts hymn, prayer, and they then would culminate with a rendition of a great hymn of the church. This is what we would call, "The Devotion" in the African American Baptist church, this soul-riveting portion of the worship experience that would galvanize the hearts and minds of God's people, which would get them prepared for the remaining portion of the service.

Even though we still embrace some of these traditions (which are not bad at all, and a practice I still look forward to), devotion is much more than a catalogue of procedures we have limited to the diaconate ministries of our churches. Devotion is more than just an act of worship; it has to do with our outlook, our identity, and the person we aspire to become. The Greek word for devotion comes from the word "*sebázomai*"; to worship religiously. *Sebázomai* denotes religious expressions of veneration in particular as well as reverential behavior in general" [40]. Devotion involves my worship, my attitude, and my behavior.

In the word "devotion," we will find the word "devote," and this means that I give all or a large portion of my time and activity to a cause or a person. So then, devotion can not be limited to just a certain time and segment in our Sunday morning or mid-week services, it has to be something that believers must consume themselves with daily. Devotion is when the believer spends time with God, and to the saint, His *Word is Revealed*, *God's Wonder is Reverenced*, and *Worship is the Response*.

The Word is Revealed: The Word of God cannot be absent from our devotion, "With my whole heart have I sought thee: O let me not wander from thy commandments" [41]. The key to having a life that is devoted to Him is to find out what it is that pleases Him! Too many times, we limit devotion to just worship, but it is His Word that influences your worship. Life that is full of worship but no word is life that will be spiritually unbalanced and spiritually unhealthy. "Devotion unites form with fire as the means by which we remain in communication with God" [42].

A. Dynasty Devotion

Family life is the foundation for the development of religious fervor in society. Devotion as a family is critical to the health of the home and the church. The church looks to the family as its original model because the family is the oldest institution. The Bible also teaches us the importance of worshiping together as a family. "And if it seem evil unto you to serve the Lord, choose you this day whom ye will serve;

whether the gods which your fathers served that *were* on the other side of the flood, or the gods of the Amorites, in whose land ye dwell: but as for me and my house, we will serve the Lord" (Joshua 24:15) [43].

There is a blessed balance when homes are united together in worship and devotion. The church and the Body of Christ are strengthened when homes are united in devotion and guided by the teachings of the Bible. Every aspect of family life should be guided by a set of principles drawn from the Bible. In order for that dynasty to thrive, moral guidance must be established in the household, not just in the Church.

Devotion as a way of life ought to be at the top of every family's list of priorities. Better churches can't be built without first building better families, because where there is no reverence for God in the house, there will be no reverence for God in the church. For our families to truly become God-centered, we must first move beyond rote religious observance. The depth of one's love for God is directly proportional to the intensity of one's devotion to Him.

B. Personal Devotion

Our personal devotion and development is what is going to determine how we affect our family devotional life and our public worship. Corporate prayer and praise is a wonderful blessing.

However, the devil always seems to find us when we're alone. In times like these, the knowledge of God's Word and the experiences of the believers will be put to the test. Your time invested in spiritual development, prayer, and study will pay dividends in service to God and in the heat of war.

II. Maintain Duties

A. Domiciliary Duties

To Religiously Educate Our Children

We have all heard about the "Three R's": Reading, Writing, and Arithmetic. I would like to revamp that and add another "R," and that would be "Religious Education." We have a biblical responsibility to train our children on who they are in Christ. The Bible says, "Bring them up in the nurture and admonition of the Lord" [44]. The word "nurture" comes from the Greek word *paideúō,* meaning, "the activity directed toward the moral and spiritual nurture and training of the child; to influence conscious will and action; to instruct by chastisement" [45]. This word "paideuo" is taken from the word *país;* "which means, a child in relation to descent" [46].

The word "admonish" in the Greek is *nouthesía,* which is a warning; an exhortation. *Nouthesía* is any of encouragement or reproof which leads to correct behavior" [47]. When combined with paideuo, it is instruction and training by act and discipline.

So then, the parent becomes the agent for behavior-shaping in the lives of the children, and this is only done through training and discipline at and early age. If there is to be orthopraxy in the life of the child, their must be the complementary component of orthodoxy that emanates from the parental figures. The Bible says, "Train up a child in the way he should go: And when he is old, he will not depart from it" [48].

The memory of a child is soft and fertile to receive the seeds of salvific information. Therefore, it behooves us to make sure we take every stride to invest and instill within them godly principles that will develop godly behaviors. It is better to sow the seed now when the ground is tilled than it is to wait and have to deal with the weeds and tares of waywardness.

This also suggests that if we are to religiously train our children, their teacher must be well acquainted with the lesson plan themselves. The best approach to initiate your children into godly living is to make sure that what comes out of your mouth is modeled in your mannerisms, as it is commonly claimed that all conduct is learned behavior.

To effectively minister our product, we must first feel its effects in our own lives.

B. The Desire in Our Duty

To See the Salvation of Our Kindred and Acquaintances

In Acts 16:28-34 it says, "[28] But Paul cried with a loud voice, saying, 'Do thyself no harm: for we are all here.' [29] Then he called for a light, and sprang in, and came trembling, and fell down before Paul and Silas, [30] And brought them out, and said, 'Sirs, what must I do to be saved?' [31] And they said, 'Believe on the Lord Jesus Christ, and thou shalt be saved, and thy house.' [32] And they spake unto him of the Lord, and to all that were in his house. [33] And he took them the same hour of the night, and washed *their* stripes; and was baptized, he and all his *(family)*, straightway. [34] And when he had brought them into his house, he set meat before them, and rejoiced, believing in God with all his house" [49].

This familiar story in the life of The Apostle emits a principle I believe fits this particular portion of study. In verses 33-35, this man desired to bring salvation to his home after receiving the gospel. This man was at the point of suicide, and the messengers of the gospel intervened by speaking a word that not only affected him, but it also would be transformational to his home. The effects of salvation should produce an evangelistic desire in the hearts of the converted for others to experience this great phenomenon of the Word.

How much of a vested interest do you really have in the salvation of others? How zealous are you when it comes to seeing your communities connected to the love and grace of Christ? Too many times, we can become so preoccupied with our own endeavors that we forget to take the message of Christ to those who are in need of a message of hope in the midst of a dark time. They need to know that no matter how debauched they are in their deportment, no matter how wretched, vile, or contemptible one may be, there is still room at the Cross. The Cross becomes that great transformer where all lives can be radically renovated and shine with the glow of the gospel.

C. Our Decorum

To Walk Circumspectly in the World

Galatians 5:16-8 says, "[16] *This* I say then, Walk in the Spirit, and ye shall not fulfill the lust of the flesh. [17] For the flesh lusteth against the Spirit, and the Spirit against the flesh: and these are contrary the one to the other: so that ye cannot do the things that ye would. [18] But if ye be led of the Spirit, ye are not under the law" [50]. James 5:17 says, "Even so faith, if it hath not works, is dead, being alone." [51].

The letter the apostle Paul penned was intended to serve as a reminder to Christians that their salvation is not contingent on adhering to a set of rules or performing certain deeds. Rather, it is wholly contingent on the mercy of God. These ideas are echoed by James as well. He explains that we are not saved because of the good works of God, but rather that good acts ought to be something that results from God's mercy. It is necessary for there to be a change within us that is demonstrated in the way we live our lives for the world to recognize us as saints of God.

This identification should not be the result of our decision to adorn ourselves with religious ornaments and paraphernalia. Rather, it should be the result of our effort to walk in the Spirit, and when we walk in the Spirit, we will be led by the Spirit. It is impossible for the Holy Spirit to guide someone in a direction they are unwilling to go.

In accordance with our Covenant, how do we walk circumspectly? Paul the Apostle answers this question, "I therefore, the prisoner of the Lord, beseech you that ye walk worthy of the vocation wherewith ye are called, [2] With all lowliness and meekness, with longsuffering, forbearing one another in love; [3] Endeavouring to keep the unity of the

Spirit in the bond of peace. [4] *There is* one Body, and one Spirit, even as ye are called in one hope of your calling; [5] One Lord, one Faith, one Baptism, [6] One God and Father of all, who *is* above all, and through all, and in you all" [52].

D. To Be just in Our Dealings

Our Regard for One Another

Paul in his letter to the church at Ephesus reminded the people of God, both Jew and Gentile, that they were united together in the realm of grace. They were made brothers and sisters through the womb of the Word. Because this, there should have been no prejudiced or biased views portrayed.

There are certain people who can reach such a degree of piety and devotion that they forget, all too quickly, that the ground is leveled at the Cross. God is concerned about how we treat one another. The Cross presents the paradigm that is vertical and horizontal. There is no way there can be a genuine vertical relationship, while we at the same time, are having a skewed horizontal perspective of others who are in the covenant community with us.

E. Faithful in Our Engagements

Our Responsibilities to One Another

Paul reminds us, "Endeavouring to keep the unity of the Spirit in the bond of peace. [4] *There is* one body, and one Spirit, even as ye are called in one hope of your calling; [5] One Lord, one faith, one baptism, [6] One God and Father of all, who *is* above all, and through all, and in you all" [53].

We are charged to be faithful in keeping unity within the body. The word "endeavor" is in the present tense, which suggests that I am constantly on duty, and diligently employed to make sure nothing causes schism or fraction within the family of God. This should be every believer's desire; to cover and protect the harmony within the Body of Christ. We have a responsibility to keep unity, not uniforms. Uniforms deal with attire, whereas unity deals with our allegiant attitude. Some are so consumed with looking alike that they fail to be linked together.

F. Exemplary in Our Deportment

The apostle Paul states, "[11] And he gave some, apostles; and some, [h]prophets; and some, evangelists; and some, pastors and teachers; [12] For the perfecting of the saints, for the work of the ministry, for the edifying of the Body of Christ: [13] Till we all come in the unity of the faith, and of the knowledge of the Son of God, unto a perfect man, unto the measure of the stature of the fullness of Christ: [14] That we *henceforth* be no more children, tossed to and fro, and carried about with every wind of doctrine, by the sleight of men, *and* cunning craftiness, whereby they lie in wait to deceive" [54].

The ultimate goal, mission, and covenant is that we be guided to reach the standards of excellence. Christians have a responsibility to lead by example. This points toward maintaining a chaste and respectful lifestyle in all settings. People who are seeking to know the Savior want to see Jesus in our living rather than hear about Him from our lips. Our lives as the people of God become the very epistle that people see that should indeed manifest the characteristics of Christ since we claim to be a part of this covenant community. In essence, the covenant is designed to shape our conduct which ultimately verifies the fact that this unique relationship we have with God has an ultimate effect upon our livelihood and deportment.

G. To Avoid All Tattling, Backbiting, and Excessive Anger

The combination of backbiting, tattling, and extreme fury is an extremely dangerous recipe that can yield results which are counter-productive to the growth of God's Kingdom. According to one definition, "tattling" means, "to tell secrets: to blab, to utter or disclose in gossip or conversation" [55]. One definition of "backbiting" is "to utter harsh or spiteful things about" [56]. When it comes to spreading rumors and pulling down fellow Kingdom residents, tattling and backbiting are cousins. When a person joins a church, he or she agrees to uphold the covenant principle of not spreading malicious rumors about other members of the congregation. In the worst possible way, this offense shatters harmony within the family. For example, one of the six items listed as things the Lord detests in Proverbs 6:19 is "A false witness *that* speaketh lies, and he that soweth discord among brethren." [57] These two factors have the potential to spark a fire that not only results in an excessive amount of wrath, but it also results in discord, schism, and separation.

Paul writes, "Be ye angry, and sin not: let not the sun go down upon your wrath: [27] Neither give place to the devil" [58]. Getting along with others is not always easy. Perhaps this problem best exemplifies the greatest difficulty the church has today. To some extent, the difficulty of accomplishing this is puzzling. It is true that, when we can't work together, we don't feel well. If we can't even get along in church, all the exalted claims we make about who we are in Christ are moot.

The advice to get along is one that can be taken at face value. It's easier to say than to accomplish. Focusing on the trivial and the inconsequential is a common way to get off track. It's human nature to misread someone else's intentions based on their tone of speech or facial expression. A stern response may be warranted, but it should be contained. Constant effort is required for harmonious co-existence.

Similar to other situations, we require the guidance of the Holy Spirit. Anger is a natural human response to the discomfiting treatments and circumstances of life. This definition that is used by Paul is "wrath" (**parorgismós**); gen. *parorgismoú*, masc. noun from *parorgízō* (3949), to make angry, provoke to have violent or bitter anger. It also refers to the irritation, exasperation or anger to which one is provoked [59]. What this phrase indicates in its most basic sense is that you have given vent to your pent-up rage and are now acting out in a violent, bitter fashion.

In the next line, Paul explains why the devil loves it when people harvest hate and bitterness: The seeds of gossip and slander are planted by pent-up resentment. The adversarial mind-set provides an opening for the adversary. The enemy frequently uses this door as a point of entry into the house of worship.

It is God's will that the church learns to live together in a way that prepares its members for eternal life. Christian living is a foretaste of the glory of Paradise. We have had a preview of God's Kingdom, and it is because of this that we are able to be good examples to the world.

H. To Abstain from Sale/Use of Intoxicating Drinks as a Beverage

Paul teaches, "And be not drunk with wine, wherein is excess; but be filled with the Spirit" [60]. I am well aware that this is a hotly disputed topic and has been so for generations. To drink alcohol or not to drink alcohol, that is the question. There has been significant debate and division over the years regarding the proper stance to take on alcoholic beverages, especially within the Baptist faith. If the truth were to be told, I believe the misappropriation of the biblical text and the failure to fully grasp the meaning of the covenant's wording are to blame for the current state of discord.

Before I go any further with this explanation, let me be clear that I am in no way encouraging anyone to make alcoholic drinks their preferred beverage, neither am I criticizing anyone for doing so. The goal of this book and its accompanying explanation is to educate and indoctrinate the reader so that he or she may make well-informed decisions about his or her own life.

CONSUMPTION VERSUS CONTROL

Can a Baptist, Bible-believing Christian drink alcohol, or does the Bible warn against letting alcohol dictate our behavior? To provide a satisfactory response, I think it's important to first consider what the Bible says regarding drinking.

Our covenant uses the term "intoxicating" which is from the word "intoxicate" which means "to excite or stupefy by alcohol or a drug, especially to the point where physical and mental control is markedly diminished." We are given numerous admonitions and cautions to avoid getting drunk throughout the Bible. Ephesians 5:18 says, "And be not drunk with wine, wherein is excess; but be filled with the Spirit" [61]. Paul is arguing that one's morals and ethics are compromised when they are under the influence of alcohol. He is warning us about the repercussions of allowing ourselves to be manipulated or influenced by substances that can cloud our judgment. His advice is to take charge and submit to the Holy Spirit's guidance. That's the devil's plan, actually; he wants us to evade the indwelling of the Holy Spirit's transforming power by any means necessary. Christians are commanded to not allow their bodies to be "mastered" by anything (I Corinthians 6:12; 2 Peter 2:19).

Another scripture that is utilized when speaking of wine or drinking is Romans 14:21 which says, "*It is* good neither to eat flesh, nor to drink wine, nor *any thing* whereby thy brother stumbleth, or is offended, or is made weak" [62]. In a nutshell, this scripture teaches that believers are to make every effort to do those things that lead to peace and mutual up-building [63]. Paul has just reiterated in this chapter his agreement with the "strong": all things are clean. In Christ, we have freedom to eat whatever food, to celebrate (or not celebrate) the Jewish feast days. In other words, Christian liberty allows us to do anything within the bounds of the Moral Law.

Paul also goes on to say in verse 22, "²² Hast thou faith? Have *it* to thyself before God. Happy *is* he that condemneth not himself in that thing which he alloweth" [64], which shows that Paul's chief priority is clearly the spiritual integrity of the church: it is wrong to do anything that causes someone else to stumble. In fact, he says, whatever you believe about these things, keep between yourself and God [65].

Clearly, the question has not yet been resolved for the enquirer. Therefore, permit me to bring this matter to a head. However, many biblical texts warn against the dangers of becoming drunk and losing self-control. Psalms 104:14-15 says, "He causeth the grass to grow for the cattle, and herb for the service of man; that he may bring forth food out of the earth; and wine *that* maketh glad the heart of man."

When was wine consumed? Paul told Timothy, "Stop drinking only water, and use a little wine because of your stomach and your frequent illness" (1 Timothy 5:23).

The Bible sometimes portrays alcohol as something good and enjoyable.

Jesus' first miracle involved turning water into wine for a wedding celebration (John 2:3-11). The term, "wine" *(oinos)* was the common Greek word for normal wine, wine that was fermented/alcoholic. Some will argue that the wine Jesus made was not fermented, but it was merely grape juice. According to the historical information about grape juice, you are probably familiar with Welch's Grape Juice, but you may not know it has ties to the history of The United Methodist Church. In the 1800s, churches faced a dilemma. To combat the epidemic of alcoholism, The Temperance Movement advocated total abstinence from all alcohol. In celebration of The Lord's Supper though, the church filled the communion **chalice** with wine. *Thomas B. Welch developed a process for pasteurizing grape juice to keep it from fermenting.*

In the 1800s, however, that was no easy task. Raw grape juice stored at room temperature—home refrigerators were not available until 1913—naturally ferments into wine. This caused a problem for congregations not wanting to use anything containing alcohol. If grape juice was not around until the 1800s, then what was it that Jesus turned into wine? I believe the biblical text and the Greek definition speaks for themselves. The consumption of wine was a custom and was the norm, being intoxicated and under the control of it was the issue.

There is no inherent sinfulness in alcoholic beverages. A Christian must abstain completely from drunkenness and any forms of intoxication. So, I assume you want to know, what is the proper attitude for us to have? It is your call. As I said at the outset of this conversation; I am merely unpacking the text from a biblical perspective. If you choose to consume, I pray you won't let yourself be manipulated, and if you choose not to consume, I hope you won't put yourself in a position to judge those who do.

I. To Be Zealous in Efforts to Advance the Kingdom of Our Savior

"But seek ye first the Kingdom of God, and his righteousness; and all these things shall be added unto you" [66] (Matthew 6:33). A fervent eagerness or excitement, as well as a strong desire, are connoted by the word "zealous." Those of us who are a part of this covenant community have the responsibility to make it our ardent and sincere goal to serve Christ and His Kingdom in the most effective manner that is open to us. The degree to which we are motivated to give His will precedence is the factor that will determine how committed we are to His will and plan for our lives.

The word "Kingdom" can be defined as being submissive to the authority and power of the king. It denotes the supremacy and the sovereignty of God over those who have submitted to His rule. I think it's necessary for us to note that our responsibility within the covenant community is to do our best to advance The King's agenda. The word, "zealous" speaks of a burning eagerness or enthusiasm, and a desire. Those of us who are a part of this covenant community must make it our energetic and earnest desire to serve Christ and His Kingdom the best way possible. Our desire to make His will priority is what will advance His purpose and His plan.

7

The Fellowship of Our Covenant

"We further engage to watch over one another in brotherly love; to remember one another in prayer; to aid one another in sickness and distress; to cultivate Christian sympathy in feeling and Christian courtesy in speech."

Hebrews 10:23-25 admonishes, "Let us hold fast the profession of *our* faith without wavering; (for He *is* faithful that promised;) [24] And let us consider one another to provoke unto love and to good works: [25] Not forsaking the assembling of ourselves together, as the manner of some *is*; but exhorting *one another:* and so much the more, as ye see the day approaching [67].

Gathering together as the church and spending time with one another is crucial because it is by these means that we can best establish and nurture the virtues of love, prayer, service, and giving. Christians need to get together to encourage one another and grow in their faith. Some of the Hebrew recipients of this letter weren't attending worship meetings regularly, which hindered their capacity to inspire one another to do good.

When Christians get together with the goal of furthering godliness and love in the world, they have the potential to accomplish incredible things. Growing in your faith requires you to keep up consistent interactions with other Christians. This is absolutely necessary.

What do we gain from this covenant and our communion? We gain brotherly love. *Agape* love is much different than any other kind of love. It is not a feeling; it's a motivation for action that we are free to choose or reject. *Agape* is a sacrificial love that voluntarily suffers inconvenience, discomfort, and even death for the benefit of another without expecting anything in return.

As a covenant community, we are privileged and blessed to be partnered with those who practice the love of God and neighbor as the greatest commandment. It is also given to us by God. When Jesus gave us what He called, a "New Commandment" at the Last Supper by instituting the Lord's Supper, He was referring to this: John 14:34-35 says, "As I have loved you, so you must love one another; this is the New and Living Commandment that I offer to you. If you have love for one another, then everyone will be able to tell that you are my disciples." As part of the church covenant, we commit to "look over one another in brotherly love." It is imperative that we acknowledge the responsibility that comes with being responsible for the well-being of the covenant community.

The Bible instructs us to have brotherly love towards one another. How do we exemplify this love and compassion within this covenant community? There are a number of avenues mentioned in the church covenant that manifests this responsibility. To begin, we are "to remember each other in prayer; to aid each other in sickness and distress." Keep each other in your thoughts and prayers while going through difficult times.

The church is sitting on the greatest and most untapped source of power, which is prayer. This is probably accurate due to the fact that we do not have a good understanding of what may actually be achieved through prayer.

The purpose of prayer is to make our requests known to God, but it also serves as the doorway through which we enter God's presence and receive His blessings and guidance. And it is in His presence that we have the luxury of speaking with him face-to-face, laying down our worries, and becoming an intercessor for those who are unable to come to Him on their own. Prayer is just as effective even when we are unable to supply the essential resources that can aid and assist others who may find themselves in a state of distress, and even in situations where we are unable to physically be present.

Care for a person "in sickness and hardship" is at the heart of the Good Samaritan parable. According to the church covenant, members are obligated to pray for one another and offer comfort to those who are ill or experiencing emotional suffering. Those who are related to one another help one another out. That's exactly who we are.

Another tune has been added. It is with great joy that I can say, "I have been adopted into the family of God." We work to develop not only a Christian's compassion in heart but also "courtesy in speech." Kindness of speech flows naturally from a Christian's generous heart. The impact of a generous word or deed might be felt for years to come.

The Bible instructs us to build up and provide strength to others. One of the most effective ways to do this is through our words of encouragement and empowerment. Words are more than the product of the larynx being moulded by the air passing through the mouth. Never underestimate the impact of your words. By the power of His words, God created the universe (Hebrews 11:3).

We have the ability to shape reality with our words because we are created in God's image. When we speak harshly or cruelly, we might crush someone's spirit and perhaps incite them to violence. Negative words have the potential to be both corrosive and traumatic. And yet, words can also edify and give life (Proverbs 18:21; Ephesians 4:29; Romans 10:14–15).

Only humans are capable of using language to communicate to one another, unlike any other species on Earth. Being able to express oneself verbally is a special and potent talent bestowed by God.

J. The Maintaining Our Covenant

We are "to be slow to take offense, but always ready for reconcili-ation,and mindful of the rules of our Savior to secure it without delay." Our covenant reminds us that every covenant partner should be ready for reconciliation. To be ready means to be open, receptive, in a suit-able state for an activity, action, or situation; fully prepared. Ephesians 4:1-3. Paul says, "I therefore, the prisoner of the Lord, beseech you that ye walk worthy of the vocation wherewith ye are called, [2] With all lowliness and meekness, with longsuffering, forbearing one another in love; [3] Endeavouring to keep the unity of the Spirit in the bond of peace [68]. Reconciliation is at the heart of the covenant community.

To reconcile means to bring back together in harmony or accord what had been separated by hostility. The word "*katallagē* " is derived from the socio-economic sphere (cf. 1 Corinthians 7:11). It speaks in general of the restoration of a proper relationship between two parties. It refers broadly to overcoming an enmity, without specifying how this enmity is removed. In Paul's writings, *katallage* is contrasted many times with "enmity" and "alienation." To put it another way, "peace" in the Bible means the full reconciliation of God and Man. In the context of salvation, the word, "reconciliation" has a broad meaning which encompasses the removal of hostility and estrangement between God and humanity. As a result, Paul may rejoice, "Therefore, because we are justified by faith, we have peace with God through our Lord Jesus Christ" (Romans 5:1).

When we examine our current connection with God, we discover evidence of reconciliation. We as believers inside the covenant com-munity should be just as willing to reconcile our indifference within the community. Since God launched the invitation for us to be admit-ted back into the fellowship and to eradicate all enmity that formerly existed because of sin. As we have been shown kindness, it is only just that we be ready to reciprocate that same commodity when we see that perimeter of peace has been breached. Our goal should be to promote and maintain unity within the Body of Christ.

8

The Furtherance of Our Covenant

'That when we remove from this place we will, as soon as possible, unite with some other Church where we can carry out the spirit of this covenant and the principles of Gods Word."

Why is it important that Christians become active members of a local church? Why is this section of our covenant so important? It's not surprising that many Christians place a low value on church member-ship in a time when commitment is scarce. It's unfortunate that many Christians bounce around from congregation to congregation, never committing to a group of believers or submitting to the leadership of a pastor. One's commitment to a local church should be reflected in many areas of life, including public holiness, the use of one's spiritual gifts in service, financial support of the ministry, the ability to give and receive correction graciously, and regular attendance at communal worship services. Expectations are high, but so are the stakes. Faithfulness to this kind of vow is essential if the Church is to fulfill her role as Christ's representation on earth. It is really important to have a spiritual home. This world is not the place to "go at it" alone if you are on a journey for spiritual enlightenment. Within the Baptist Church, there are three ways to become a part of the covenant community.

The first way of joining the covenant community is by way of Profession of Faith or as we say, "Candidate for Baptism." This is when a person is making their first public profession of faith in Christ as Lord and Savior. And upon this confession, there is a small catechism between that pastor and the new convert about what they believe and their willingness to be submissive to the commands and principles of God's Word.

Then, there is the "Way by Letter." This was just another way of a person joining a covenant community, and a person with a letter was already a member of a local church but decided to join another assembly either because of relocation or transfer. The idea of a letter of transfer or recommendation is seen in Acts 18:27-28: "[27] And when he was disposed to pass into Achaia, the brethren wrote, exhorting the disciples to receive him: who, when he was come, helped them much which had believed through grace: [28] For he mightily convinced the Jews, *and that* publickly, shewing by the scriptures that Jesus was Christ" [69]. This method provides an account of stewardship and provides knowledge to that pastor and church so that they may know who is being admitted into the fellowship.

The third way into the fellowship is through "Statement of Christian Experience" or "By Christian Experience." This option is for those who are neither making a first-time profession of faith nor coming from another church. New members in this category are simply saying, "I'm not a new Christian, and I don't have a current church membership, but I want to be a member of this church."

In conclusion, it is important to keep in mind that the church covenant is not the Word of God; rather, the Word of God serves as the basis for and the primary influence in the church covenant. It is my hope and prayer that Baptist churches will once again rekindle a desire to be guided by the principles of our church covenant, so that they can enjoy the full benefits offered within a covenant community.

End Notes

[1] *The Holy Bible: King James Version.* (1995). (electronic ed. of the 1769 edition of the 1611 Authorized Version., Ro 8:14). Bellingham WA: Logos Research Systems, Inc.

[2] Louw, J. P., & Nida, E. A. (1996). *Greek-English lexicon of the New Testament: based on semantic domains* (electronic ed. of the 2nd edition., Vol. 1, p. 464). New York: United Bible Societies.

[3] Torrey, R. A. (1910). *The person and work of the Holy Spirit as revealed in the Scriptures and in personal experience* (p. 7). New York; Chicago: Fleming H. Revell.

[4] Patterson, P. (2003). Baptism. In C. Brand, C. Draper, A. England, S. Bond, E. R. Clendenen, & T. C. Butler (Eds.), *Holman Illustrated Bible Dictionary* (p. 166). Nashville, TN: Holman Bible Publishers.

[5] Zodhiates, S. (2000). *The complete word study dictionary: New Testament* (electronic ed.). Chattanooga, TN: AMG Publisher.

[6] *The Holy Bible: King James Version.* (2009). (Electronic Edition of the 1900 Authorized Version., Mt. 3:5 7). Bellingham, WA: Logos Research Systems, Inc.

[7] *The Holy Bible: King James Version.* (1995). (electronic ed. of the 1769 edition of the 1611 Authorized Version., Mt 3:15). Bellingham WA: Logos Research Systems, Inc.

[8] *The New International Version.* (2011). (Is 53:12). Grand Rapids, MI: Zondervan.

[9] *The Holy Bible: King James Version.* (2009). (Electronic Edition of the 1900 Authorized Version., Ps 121:4). Bellingham, WA: Logos Research Systems, Inc.

[10] *The Holy Bible: King James Version.* (2009). (Electronic Edition of the 1900 Authorized Version., Ps 46:1). Bellingham, WA: Logos Research Systems, Inc.

[11] *The Holy Bible: King James Version.* (2009). (Electronic Edition of the 1900 Authorized Version., Mt 18:15 17). Bellingham, WA: Logos Research Systems, Inc.

[12] *The Holy Bible: King James Version.* (2009). (Electronic Edition of the 1900 Authorized Version., Ac 5:1–11). Bellingham, WA: Logos Research Systems, Inc.

[13] *The Holy Bible: English Standard Version.* (2016). (Ps 100:1–5). Wheaton, IL: Crossway Bibles.

[14] Strong, T. (2003). Paraclete. In C. Brand, C. Draper, A. England, S. Bond, E. R. Clendenen, & T. C. Butler (Eds.), *Holman Illustrated Bible Dictionary* (p. 1247). Nashville, TN: Holman Bible Publishers.

[15] *The Holy Bible: King James Version.* (2009). (Electronic Edition of the 1900 Authorized Version., Jn 14:16–18). Bellingham, WA: Logos Research Systems, Inc.

[16] *The Holy Bible: King James Version.* (2009). (Electronic Edition of the 1900 Authorized Version., 1 Jn 4:7). Bellingham, WA: Logos Research Systems, Inc.

[17] *The Holy Bible: King James Version.* (2009). (Electronic Edition of the 1900 Authorized Version., 1 Jn 4:7). Bellingham, WA: Logos Research Systems, Inc.

[18] *The Holy Bible: King James Version.* (2009). (Electronic Edition of the 1900 Authorized Version., 1 Jn 3:14). Bellingham, WA: Logos Research Systems, Inc.

[19] Youngblood, R. F., Bruce, F. F., & Harrison, R. K., Thomas Nelson Publishers (Eds.). (1995). *In Nelson's new illustrated Bible dictionary.* Nashville, TN: Thomas Nelson, Inc.

[20] *The Holy Bible: King James Version.* (2009). (Electronic Edition of the 1900 Authorized Version., Col 1:9–10). Bellingham, WA: Logos Research Systems, Inc.

[21] Cabal Ted. (2003). Holy. In C. Brand, C. Draper, A. England, S. Bond, E. R. Clendenen, & T. C. Butler (Eds.), *Holman Illustrated Bible Dictionary* (p. 772). Nashville, TN: Holman Bible Publishers.

[22] *The Holy Bible: King James Version.* (2009). (Electronic Edition of the 1900 Authorized Version., 2 Co 7:1). Bellingham, WA: Logos Research Systems, Inc.

[23] *The Holy Bible: King James Version.* (2009). (Electronic Edition of the 1900 Authorized Version., 1 Th 4:18). Bellingham, WA: Logos Research Systems, Inc.

[24] *The Holy Bible: King James Version.* (2009). (Electronic Edition of the 1900 Authorized Version., Ac 2:44–47). Bellingham, WA: Logos Research Systems, Inc.

[25] *The Holy Bible: King James Version.* (2009). (Electronic Edition of the 1900 Authorized Version., Jos 1:8). Bellingham, WA: Logos Research Systems, Inc.

[26] Merriam-Webster, I. (2003). *Merriam-Webster's collegiate dictionary.* (Eleventh ed.). Springfield, MA: Merriam-Webster, Inc.

[27] Nelson, D. P. (2003). Worship. In C. Brand, C. Draper, A. England, S. Bond, E. R. Clendenen, & T. C. Butler (Eds.), *Holman Illustrated Bible Dictionary* (pp. 1686–1687). Nashville, TN: Holman Bible Publishers.

[28] Clendenen, E. R. with York Hershael W. (2003). Discipline. In C. Brand, C. Draper, A. England, S. Bond, E. R. Clendenen, & T. C. Butler (Eds.), *Holman Illustrated Bible Dictionary* (p. 426). Nashville, TN: Holman Bible Publishers.

[29] Mohler, R. A., Jr. (2003). Doctrine. In C. Brand, C. Draper, A. England, S. Bond, E. R. Clendenen, & T. C. Butler (Eds.), *Holman Illustrated Bible Dictionary* (p. 436). Nashville, TN: Holman Bible Publishers.

[30] Mohler, R. A., Jr. (2003). Doctrine. In C. Brand, C. Draper, A. England, S. Bond, E. R. Clendenen, & T. C. Butler (Eds.), *Holman Illustrated Bible Dictionary* (p. 436). Nashville, TN: Holman Bible Publishers.

[31] *The Holy Bible: King James Version.* (2009). (Electronic Edition of the 1900 Authorized Version., 2 Co 9:7). Bellingham, WA: Logos Research Systems, Inc.

[32] *The Holy Bible: King James Version.* (2009). (Electronic Edition of the 1900 Authorized Version., 1 Ti 6:10). Bellingham, WA: Logos Research Systems, Inc.

[33] *The Holy Bible: King James Version.* (2009). (Electronic Edition of the 1900 Authorized Version., Hag 1:2–6). Bellingham, WA: Logos Research Systems, Inc.

[34] *The Holy Bible: King James Version.* (2009). (Electronic Edition of the 1900 Authorized Version., 1 Co 9:9–10). Bellingham, WA: Logos Research Systems, Inc.

[35] The Holy Bible: King James Version. (2009). (Electronic Edition of the 1900 Authorized Version., Mt 25:40). Bellingham, WA: Logos Research Systems, Inc.

[36] *The Holy Bible: King James Version.* (2009). (Electronic Edition of the 1900 Authorized Version., Mt 28:19–20). Bellingham, WA: Logos Research Systems, Inc.

[37] *The Holy Bible: King James Version.* (2009). (Electronic Edition of the 1900 Authorized Version., Jn 14:12). Bellingham, WA: Logos Research Systems, Inc.

[38] Zodhiates, S. (2000). *The complete word study dictionary: New Testament* (electronic ed.). Chattanooga, TN: AMG Publishers.

[39] William C. Turner, *Disciple for African American Christians A Journey through the Church Covenant,* (Valley Forge, PA, Judson Press 2002), 67

[40] Zodhiates, S. (2000). *The complete word study dictionary: New Testament* (electronic ed.). Chattanooga, TN: AMG Publishers.

[41] *The Holy Bible: King James Version.* (2009). (Electronic Edition of the 1900 Authorized Version., Ps 119:10). Bellingham, WA: Logos Research Systems, Inc.

[42] Ibid., 67

[43] *The Holy Bible: King James Version.* (2009). (Electronic Edition of the 1900 Authorized Version., Jos 24:15). Bellingham, WA: Logos Research Systems, Inc.

[44] *The Holy Bible: King James Version.* (2009). (Electronic Edition of the 1900 Authorized Version., Eph 6:4). Bellingham, WA: Logos Research Systems, Inc.

[45] Zodhiates, S. (2000). *The complete word study dictionary: New Testament* (electronic ed.). Chattanooga, TN: AMG Publishers.

[46] Zodhiates, S. (2000). *The complete word study dictionary: New Testament* (electronic ed.). Chattanooga, TN: AMG Publishers.

[47] Zodhiates, S. (2000). *The complete word study dictionary: New Testament* (electronic ed.). Chattanooga, TN: AMG Publishers.

[48] *The Holy Bible: King James Version.* (2009). (Electronic Edition of the 1900 Authorized Version., Pr 22:6). Bellingham, WA: Logos Research Systems, Inc.

[49] *The Holy Bible: King James Version.* (2009). (Electronic Edition of the 1900 Authorized Version., Ac 16:28–34). Bellingham, WA: Logos Research Systems, Inc.

[50] *The Holy Bible: King James Version.* (2009). (Electronic Edition of the 1900 Authorized Version., Ga 5:16–18). Bellingham, WA: Logos Research Systems, Inc.

[51] The Holy Bible: King James Version. (2009). (Electronic Edition of the 1900 Authorized Version., Jas 2:17). Bellingham, WA: Logos Research Systems, Inc.

[52] *The Holy Bible: King James Version.* (2009). (Electronic Edition of the 1900 Authorized Version., Eph 4:1–6). Bellingham, WA: Logos Research Systems, Inc.

[53] *The Holy Bible: King James Version.* (2009). (Electronic Edition of the 1900 Authorized Version., Eph 4:3–7). Bellingham, WA: Logos Research Systems, Inc.'

[54] *The Holy Bible: King James Version.* (2009). (Electronic Edition of the 1900 Authorized Version., Eph 4:11–14). Bellingham, WA: Logos Research Systems, Inc.

[55] Merriam-Webster, I. (2003). *In Merriam-Webster's collegiate dictionary.* (Eleventh ed.). Merriam-Webster, Inc.

[56] Merriam-Webster, I. (2003). *In Merriam-Webster's collegiate dictionary.* (Eleventh ed.). Merriam-Webster, Inc.

[57] *The Holy Bible: King James Version* (Electronic Edition of the 1900 Authorized Version., Pr 6:19). (2009). Logos Research Systems, Inc.

[58] *The Holy Bible: King James Version* (Electronic Edition of the 1900 Authorized Version., Eph 4:26–27). (2009). Logos Research Systems, Inc.

[59] Zodhiates, S. (2000). *In The complete word study dictionary: New Testament* (electronic ed.). AMG Publishers.

[60] *The Holy Bible: King James Version* (Electronic Edition of the 1900 Authorized Version., Eph 5:18). (2009). Logos Research Systems, Inc.

[61] *The Holy Bible: King James Version* (Electronic Edition of the 1900 Authorized Version., Eph 5:17–19). (2009). Logos Research Systems, Inc.

[62] *The Holy Bible: King James Version* (Electronic Edition of the 1900 Authorized Version., Ro 14:21). (2009). Logos Research Systems, Inc.

[63] Mounce, R. H. (1995). *Romans* (Vol. 27, p. 257). Broadman & Holman Publishers.

[64] *The Holy Bible: King James Version* (Electronic Edition of the 1900 Authorized Version., Ro 14:22–23). (2009). Logos Research Systems, Inc.

[65] Boa, K., & Kruidenier, W. (2000). *Romans* (Vol. 6, p. 428). Broadman & Holman Publishers.

[66] *The Holy Bible: King James Version* (Electronic Edition of the 1900 Authorized Version., Mt 6:33). (2009). Logos Research Systems, Inc.

[67] *The Holy Bible: King James Version* (Electronic Edition of the 1900 Authorized Version., Heb 10:23–25). (2009). Logos Research Systems, Inc.

[68] *The Holy Bible: King James Version* (Electronic Edition of the 1900 Authorized Version., Eph 4:1–3). (2009). Logos Research Systems, Inc.

[69] *The Holy Bible: King James Version* (Electronic Edition of the 1900 Authorized Version., Ac 18:27–28). (2009). Logos Research Systems, In